EXPLORING SPACE
AND BEYOND

FUTURE
EXPLORERS

ROBOTS IN
SPACE

by Steve Kortenkamp

CAPSTONE PRESS
a capstone imprint

Connect Books are published by Capstone Press,
1710 Roe Crest Drive, North Mankato, Minnesota 56003
www.capstonepub.com

Library of Congress Cataloging-in-Publication Data
Kortenkamp, Steve, author.
  Future explorers : robots in space / Steve Kortenkamp.
     pages cm. — (Exploring space and beyond)
  Summary: "Describes the use of robots in space"—Provided by publisher.
  Audience: Ages 8–14.
  Audience: Grades 4 to 6.
  Includes bibliographical references and index.
  ISBN 978-1-4914-4163-3 (library binding)
  ISBN 978-1-4914-4177-0 (paperback)
  ISBN 978-1-4914-4183-1 (eBook PDF)
  1. Space robotics—Juvenile literature. 2. Space probes—Juvenile literature.
  3. Outer space—Exploration—Juvenile literature. I. Title. II. Title: Robots in
space.
  TL1097.K667 2016
  629.43'5—dc23
                                2015017739

Editorial Credits
Abby Colich, editor; Kyle Grenz, designer; Wanda Winch, media researcher;
Tori Abraham, production specialist

Photo Credits
ESA: MPS for OSIRIS Team, MPS/UPD/LAM/IAA/RSSD/INTA/UPM/
DASP/IDA, 27, Rosetta/NavCam, 41; Getty Images: SSPL, 14, The LIFE Picture
Collection/NASA, 13; NASA, 15, APL/JHU/NEAR Project, 38, Goddard Space
Flight Center, Conceptual Image Lab, 45, Johns Hopkins University Applied
Physics Laboratory/Carnegie Institution of Washington, 31, JPL, 19 (bottom), 44,
JPL/Cornell University, 22-23, JPL/KSC, 6, JPL/University of Arizona, 16 (top),
33, JPL-Caltech, 7, 21, JPL-Caltech/Cornell University/Arizona State University,
10-11, JPL-Caltech/MSSS, 25, JPL-Caltech/MSSS and PSI, 28-29, JPL-Caltech/
University of Arizona, 26, JPL-Caltech/University of Arizona/Texas A&M
University, 8-9, JPL-Caltech/University of Arizona/University of Idaho, 34, JSC,
Cover (front), 43, NSSDC Photo Gallery, 16-17 (bottom), 19 (top), Scott Andrews/
Canon, 5; Science Source: 36-37, NASA, 37 (top); Shutterstock: clearviewstock,
space element, Songquan Deng, 5 (right)

Printed in the United States of America in Stevens Point, Wisconsin
032015   008824WZF15

Table of Contents

CHAPTER 1

What Are Space Robots?

With a bright and thundering liftoff, a tall white rocket soars into space. The rocket is carrying a six-wheeled robot named *Curiosity*. On August 5, 2012, nine months after leaving Earth, *Curiosity* touches down on the planet Mars. It begins exploring the red planet.

Scientists sent *Curiosity* to Mars to help them answer questions about the planet. Did Mars once have rivers, lakes, and oceans like Earth? Was there ever anything living on Mars? Will people be able to live on Mars someday? The U.S. space agency NASA builds robots and sends them into space to help answer these and other questions.

NASA launched the *Curiosity* rover on November 26, 2011.

WHAT IS NASA?

NASA stands for National Aeronautics and Space Administration. It is a part of the United States government. Almost 60,000 people work for NASA. Only a few of these workers are the astronauts who go into space. Most of NASA's workers are scientists, engineers, lawyers, writers, or teachers. They work at many universities and at NASA centers around the country.

Kennedy Space Center Headquarters in Merritt Island, Florida

Fact

Robots don't just explore outer space. They explore dangerous places on Earth such as volcanoes and the ocean floor. They also work in factories making everything from candy bars to cars and trucks and even other robots.

A robot is any kind of machine that can perform the tasks that people give it. Space robots are sent on missions to places that are too dangerous or too far away for an astronaut to visit. Space robots carry cameras, telescopes, microscopes, and other equipment.

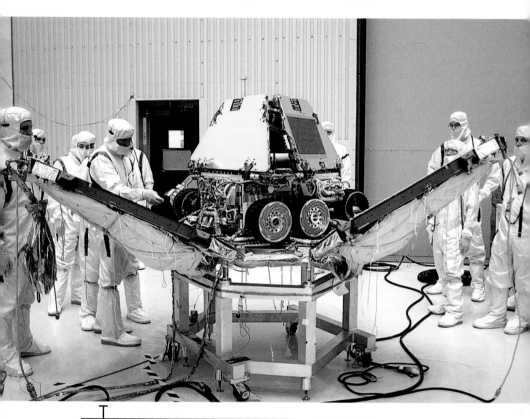

NASA technicians work on the landing gear of a Mars rover.

Scientists on Earth use computers to program the space robots so they can perform different tasks. These tasks include taking pictures, collecting samples of soil, or analyzing rocks. Using their own computers, the robots then send all of the images and other information back to scientists on Earth.

Scientist Katie Stack Morgan examines Mars rover images on her computer.

Fact

The total cost of building *Curiosity*, launching it into space, and operating it on Mars is very high. NASA will have spent more than $2.5 billion on the mission, from the earliest planning in 2003 until the end of the mission in 2026.

Scientists work together with engineers to write a plan for how to design a space robot. They send their plans to NASA. Then they ask the space agency to build the robot and launch it into space.

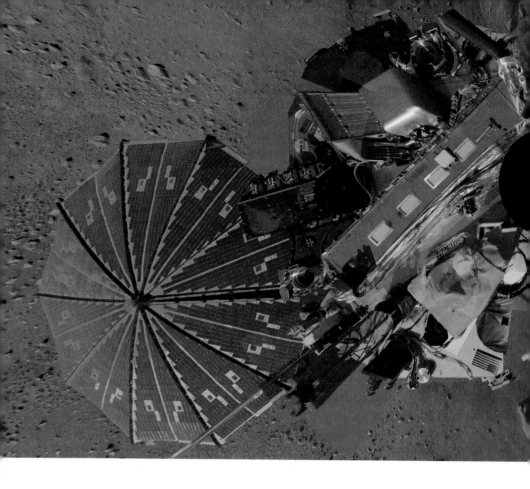

NASA builds two kinds of space robots that reach the surfaces of objects in space—**landers** and **rovers**. Landers are robots that touch down on a surface to study rocks, ice, and soil. A lander can only study the area directly around where it lands. A lander can't move around after it touches down.

Rovers use wheels to explore a larger area on a planet's surface. If scientists want to study a strange-looking rock on Mars, they have two ways of telling the rover to drive to the rock. Engineers can send commands to the rover telling it exactly where to go. For example, "Go straight for 10 feet (3 meters); stop; turn left; drive straight 5 feet (1.5 m); stop at rock." The second method is to give the rover a target and allow it to find the best route. With automatic driving, the robot uses its computer brain to avoid obstacles.

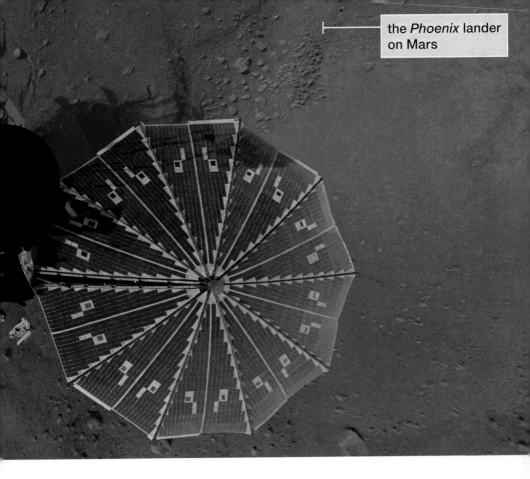

the *Phoenix* lander on Mars

Other types of space robots stay in space instead of landing on a surface. **Orbiters** can circle around planets and other objects. An orbiter circles an object in space and gathers information for many years. Robot flyby missions pass an object in space without orbiting or landing. Flyby missions only study an object for a few days as they fly past.

lander—a spacecraft that lands on an object to study the surface

rover—a small vehicle moved by remote control

orbiter—a spacecraft that orbits a planet or other space objects

9

It is a lot easier to send a robot into space than it is to send a person. That's because robots don't need food, water, or air. All they need is power. They use electricity to power their equipment and to send information back to scientists on Earth.

How a robot gets power depends on how it is built. Robots that don't need a lot of power are built with **solar panels**. Solar panels turn sunlight into electricity. But solar-powered robots only work when they are in bright sunlight. If dirt or dust blocks the solar panels of a lander or rover, then the robot won't work. Sometimes this happens to rovers on Mars. Scientists must wait for strong winds to blow the dust off. Then the solar panels start making power again.

solar panel—a flat surface that collects sunlight and turns it into power

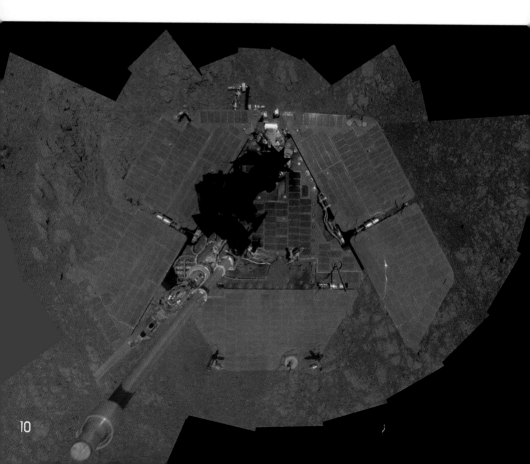

A big rover such as *Curiosity* needs a lot of power for driving around and operating all of its equipment. Scientists also need it to keep working when it is covered in dust. That's why they built *Curiosity* to use **nuclear** power. Inside a nuclear **generator**, tiny **atoms** split apart and give off a lot of heat. In *Curiosity* some of the heat changes into electricity to power the rover.

nuclear—having to do with the energy created by splitting atoms

generator—a machine that converts energy into electricity

atom—a piece of matter in its smallest form

The photo on the left shows the rover *Opportunity*'s solar panels covered in dust. The photo on the right, taken two months later, shows the solar panels clean.

CHAPTER 2

Robots on Mars

For more than 400 years, people have been asking if there is life on Mars. To find out, scientists began by studying life on Earth. They know that all life on Earth needs water. So scientists started using robots to search Mars for signs of water.

In 1964 the first close-up pictures ever taken of Mars came from the *Mariner 4* flyby mission. The *Mariner 4* cameras showed clouds in Mars' **atmosphere**. This was the first sign of water. But scientists couldn't tell if anything was alive on the surface.

In 1971 NASA sent the *Mariner 9* orbiter to get more and better pictures. *Mariner 9* sent back pictures of huge volcanoes and a giant canyon. The canyon stretches one-fourth of the way around Mars. It is far wider and deeper than the Grand Canyon in Arizona, the biggest canyon on Earth. Like the Grand Canyon, the giant canyon on Mars looks as though it was created by flowing water.

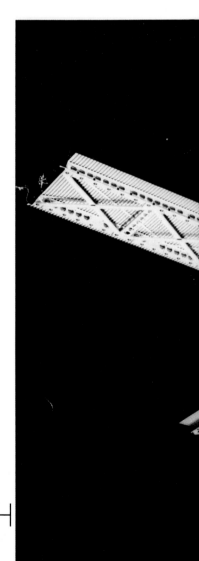

atmosphere—the layer of gases that surrounds some planets, dwarf planets, and moons

The *Mariner 9* was the first space robot to orbit another planet.

Using the *Mariner 9* orbiter, scientists also discovered dried-up rivers and lakes. Pictures from *Mariner 9* proved that Mars was once a very wet planet. But now the surface of Mars appeared to be dry. To figure out what happened to all the water and to keep searching for life, scientists built new robots to land on Mars.

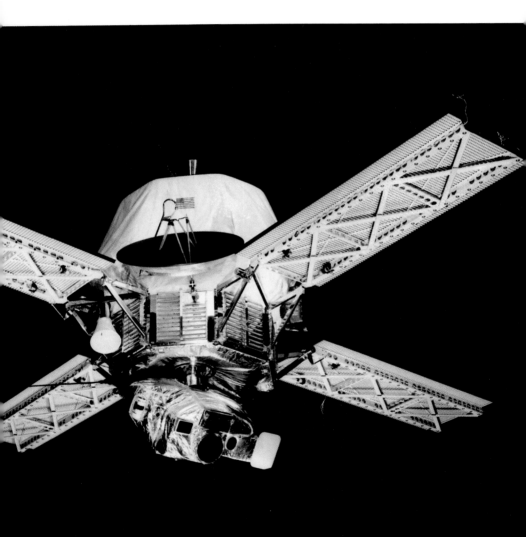

After *Mariner 9* scientists sent four more robots to Mars in 1976. These four robots were part of twin *Viking* missions, called *Viking 1* and *Viking 2*. When the *Viking* missions got to Mars, they each transformed into two different robots, an orbiter and a lander. The two solar-powered *Viking* orbiters stayed in space, circling around Mars. They took pictures of its surface. Meanwhile, the two nuclear-powered *Viking* landers used parachutes and small rockets to gently touch down on opposite sides of the planet.

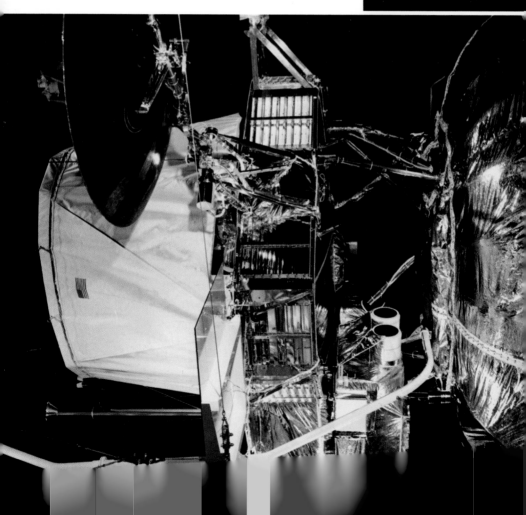

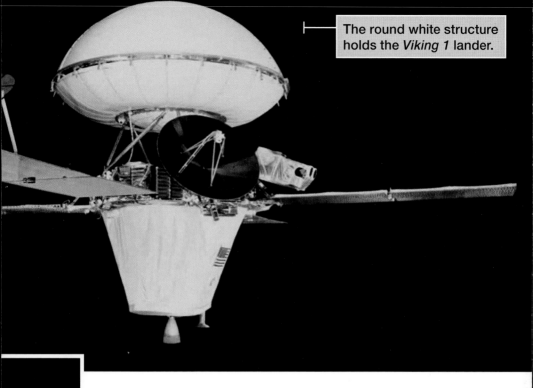

The round white structure holds the *Viking 1* lander.

The *Viking* orbiters sent pictures of Mars back to curious scientists on Earth. The pictures showed teardrop-shaped islands and other interesting patterns on Mars' surface. The scientists realized these things meant that huge floods of water must have once moved across Mars. Other pictures showed more dried-up rivers. This could mean that rain once fell on Mars. Most surprising of all were pictures that seemed to show shorelines of ancient oceans. These oceans may have once covered over half of the red planet. The *Viking* orbiters also took pictures of the ice caps that cover the north and south **poles** of Mars.

Fact
Mars is often called the red planet because of the color of its surface.

Viking spacecraft

pole—the northernmost or southernmost point on a planet

In 1976 scientists also got their first glimpse from the two *Viking* landers of what Mars looks like on the ground. They didn't see any life at all. No trees or bushes or grass. No birds or snakes or insects. In all directions, as far as the robots could see, there were only rocks and sand.

a display featuring the *Viking* lander

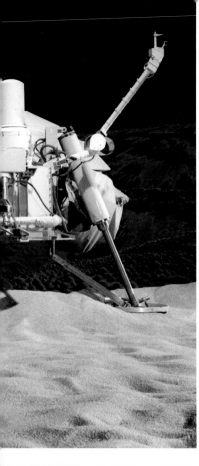

Scientists who had dreamed of finding life on Mars were disappointed. But they didn't give up. They wanted to send robots that could move around on Mars. These robots would be able to pick up some of the rocks. They wanted to look underneath the rocks and inside them for signs of water or life. To do this, NASA started building rovers that could drive around and explore larger areas of Mars.

Fact
More robot missions have been sent to explore Mars than any other planet in our solar system. More than 40 different missions have been launched, but more than half of them failed.

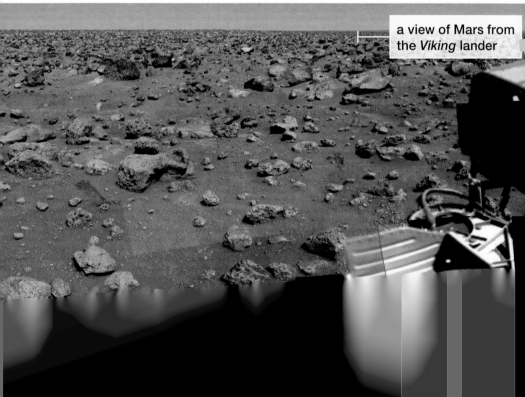

a view of Mars from the *Viking* lander

CHAPTER 3

Rise of the Rover Robots

On July 4, 1997, NASA's tiny solar-powered robot *Sojourner* became the first rover to land on Mars. *Sojourner* weighed only 23 pounds (10 kilograms). It was about the size of a small red wagon. It had cameras and other instruments, but its real mission was to test a new way of landing space robots. Instead of using rockets to gently touch down as on the *Viking* landers, scientists built *Sojourner* with 24 airbags around it.

When they were inflated, the airbags looked like big white balloons. Safely nestled inside the airbags, *Sojourner* bounced along the surface before rolling to a stop. Next the airbags deflated and opened up like petals of a flower. Scientists sent a signal from Earth telling *Sojourner* to wake up. Then it drove off of the airbags and onto the rocky surface of Mars. The airbag landing test worked perfectly.

Sojourner with deflated airbags after landing on Mars

Sojourner airbags during testing in June 1995

19

In 2004 NASA landed identical twin rovers named *Spirit* and *Opportunity* on Mars. These twin rovers are much bigger than *Sojourner*. They weigh 400 pounds (180 kg) each. Both are solar powered. They used airbags to land on opposite sides of Mars. *Spirit* and *Opportunity* each have nine cameras. Scientists use these cameras to drive the rovers and to study rocks, soil, and the atmosphere on Mars. Each rover also has a robot arm that holds a microscope and a tool for scraping rocks. Scientists can scrape small holes into rocks and then use the rover's microscope to study **minerals** inside the rocks. Using *Spirit* and *Opportunity*, scientists have discovered minerals on Mars that can only form in water. This led scientists to believe there was once water on Mars.

mineral—a solid substance often found in rocks or soil

Spirit's robotic arm on Mars on October 11, 2009

In 2009, after driving almost 5 miles (8 kilometers) across the surface of Mars, the small wheels of *Spirit* suddenly became stuck in sand. NASA's engineers tried everything they could think of to free *Spirit*, but nothing worked. The rover couldn't move to face its solar panels toward the sun. Without enough power to operate, *Spirit* eventually stopped sending information back to Earth. NASA received the last signal from *Spirit* on March 22, 2010. If humans someday travel to Mars, they may find *Spirit* waiting for them in the sand.

Opportunity snapped this shot of a rock wall on Mars that scientists call Burns Cliff.

Scientists are having more luck with *Opportunity.* At first NASA only planned to use the rover for 90 days. But the mission has been extended many times. Scientists have been driving it around the planet for more than 11 years. *Opportunity* has traveled over 26 miles (42 km) since it landed. And it's still going. *Opportunity* has helped scientists learn more about the surface of Mars.

Mars is over 13,000 miles (20,000 km) all the way around. That's more than half the size of Earth. *Opportunity* can't explore Mars by itself. So NASA built an even bigger rover and sent it to a very interesting place on the red planet.

NASA began planning for the *Curiosity* rover mission in 2003. Nearly 4,000 people spent about nine years designing and building the robot and the equipment it carries. Scientists and engineers around the world built different parts for the rover. They then sent them to NASA's Jet Propulsion Laboratory in Pasadena, California.

Engineers in Pasadena assembled all the parts and tested the rover. Once they knew it could work properly, they carefully packed *Curiosity* on a giant plane. The plane flew the rover to NASA's Kennedy Space Center in Florida. At the space center, workers placed the rover on the rocket that would take it to Mars. On November 26, 2011, NASA launched *Curiosity*.

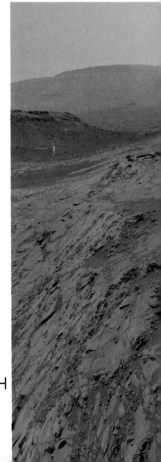

Curiosity took this 360-degree panoramic self-portrait from Mars.

Curiosity is the biggest rover ever sent into space. It is more than 7 feet (2 m) tall and about 10 feet (3 m) long. It weighs nearly 2,000 pounds (900 kg). That's about the size of a pickup truck. Scientists didn't want *Curiosity* to get stuck in sand like *Spirit*, so they gave it much bigger wheels. In fact, each of *Curiosity*'s six wheels is as big as the entire *Sojourner* rover. *Curiosity* is so big that the airbag landing used for the other Mars rovers would have failed. The airbags would have popped during landing. So scientists designed a new kind of landing using a rocket sky crane. The sky crane lowered the rover on long cables and gently set it down. Once on the ground, *Curiosity* cut the cables with small blades. The sky crane flew off and crash-landed about 0.5 mile (0.8 km) away.

NASA sent *Curiosity* to Gale crater on Mars. Gale crater is nearly 100 miles (160 km) across. It formed over 3 billion years ago when an **asteroid** smashed into Mars. Long ago water filled the crater, forming a huge lake. Over billions of years, bits of dirt flowed into the lake. These bits of dirt settled to the bottom of the lake, forming layers of mud. A thin layer of mud formed every year. When Mars began to dry up, the layers of mud in Gale crater turned into layers of rock.

Now the layers of rock in Gale crater are like time capsules. Each layer of rock holds clues about what Mars was like long ago when that layer first formed. Scientists sent *Curiosity* into Gale crater to study these layers of rock to search for clues about water and life on Mars in the past.

asteroid—a large rock that travels through space

Gale crater

Curiosity captured this shot as it traveled across Mars.

This image of Mars shows where *Curiosity* explored Gale crater.

Curiosity has many pieces of equipment that scientists are using to study Mars. There are 10 cameras on the rover. Four of these cameras are underneath the body to help the rover avoid hitting rocks or falling into big cracks. The rover also has a robot arm with tools for drilling into rocks. It has a microscope for studying minerals. *Curiosity*'s head, called a mast, has cameras that look like two eyes. It has lasers for burning holes into rocks that are too far away to reach with its arm. Inside the body of *Curiosity* is a science laboratory. The laboratory can perform chemistry experiments. It has an X-ray machine for studying rocks. The robot arm drops small samples of rocks and soil into the laboratory so scientists can study them.

rocks on Mars (below) seen next to rocks from a stream on Earth (opposite page)

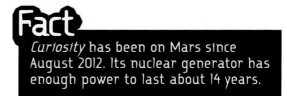

One of the first discoveries scientists made with *Curiosity* occurred when it landed in an old dried-up stream. Water flowing in the stream had left layers of pebbles that were rounded by **erosion**. Scientists compared pictures of these rounded pebbles on Mars with streams on Earth. They learned that the water in the stream must have flowed for many years. Streams like this on Earth are filled with living things. Scientists are using *Curiosity* to search around the dried-up stream for signs that anything was alive. They have yet to discover any signs of life.

erosion—wearing away of rock or soil by wind, water, or ice

CHAPTER 4

Exploring Other Planets and Moons

Mars is an exciting place to study, but it isn't the only planet that scientists are exploring with space robots. In fact, NASA has sent robots to every single planet in our solar system. In 2011 scientists sent a solar-powered orbiter named *Messenger* to Mercury. *Messenger* discovered volcanoes on the planet. Using information from *Messenger*, scientists are learning more about Mercury's huge iron **core**. The orbiter is also exploring ice hiding in craters at the south pole of Mercury. After four years of studying Mercury, the *Messenger* robot finally ran out of fuel and crashed into the planet on April 30, 2015. It became the first robot to ever reach the surface of Mercury.

Venus is sometimes called Earth's twin planet. But several orbiters and landers that NASA and the Russian space agency sent there show that Venus is very different from Earth. A thick atmosphere blankets the entire planet with clouds that rain acid. The atmosphere traps so much heat that the surface is hot enough to melt some metals. Temperatures on Venus get above 850°F (450°C). Landers sent to the surface only survived a few minutes. They sent back just a few pictures before they were crushed like tin cans by the weight of the atmosphere and fried by the extreme heat and acid.

core—the inner part of a planet or dwarf planet that is made of metal or rock

This photo of a mountain inside a large crater on Mercury was one of the last taken by *Messenger*.

NASA sent a very complex nuclear-powered orbiter named *Galileo* to Jupiter in 1995. *Galileo* visited Jupiter with a little **probe** riding along its back. NASA sent commands to drop the small probe into the atmosphere of Jupiter to study clouds on the giant planet. As the probe slowly dropped through the clouds on a parachute, it sent information up to *Galileo*. Then *Galileo* sent the information back to scientists on Earth. They discovered that Jupiter's atmosphere contains the gases argon, krypton, and xenon.

Scientists also used the *Galileo* orbiter to study the giant moons of Jupiter. Pictures of the moon Io show volcanoes erupting molten rock into space. Using *Galileo*, scientists now know that some material from Io's volcanoes falls onto Jupiter's atmosphere, creating colorful bands of light. They also discovered that the moon Europa has an ocean of water hidden under a thin crust of ice. The ocean may be more than 60 miles (100 km) deep. Many scientists now wonder if any creatures are living in that ocean. They are working with NASA to design new robot submarines that can melt through Europa's frozen crust and explore the ocean below.

probe—a small vehicle used to explore objects in outer space

Galileo's camera took this shot of Jupiter's volcanic moon Io.

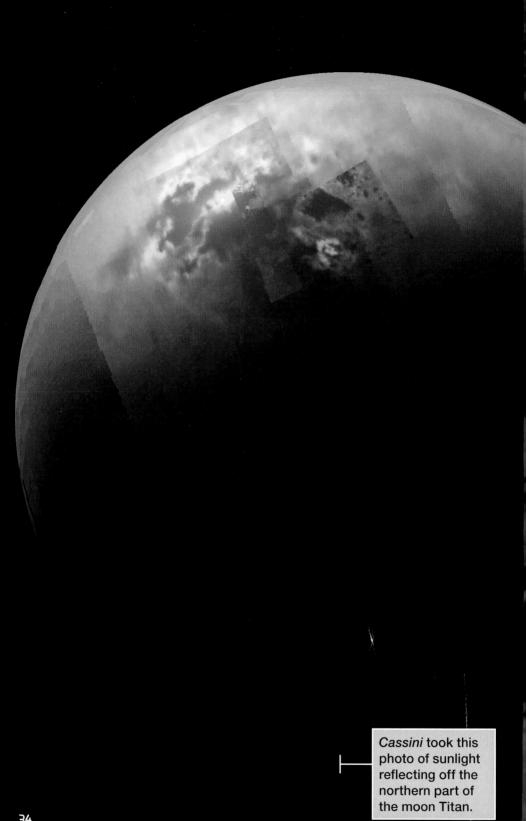

Cassini took this photo of sunlight reflecting off the northern part of the moon Titan.

NASA's *Cassini* orbiter traveled through space for seven years before arriving at Saturn on July 1, 2004. It carried a lander on its back the entire way. Scientists are using *Cassini* to study Saturn's rings and to explore some of its 60 moons. When *Cassini* arrived at Saturn, NASA sent commands to drop the lander onto a very interesting moon named Titan. Titan has an atmosphere just like Earth's. The lander used parachutes to slowly fall to the surface. As it was dropping, it sent pictures back to *Cassini*. Then *Cassini* sent the pictures back to scientists on Earth. The pictures show that Titan has streams, rivers, and lakes. But Titan is much too cold for liquid water. It is about −290°F (−180°C). Instead of water, scientists discovered that on Titan it rains a liquid called methane that fills the rivers and lakes.

VENUS WAS FIRST

Although Mars has fascinated people for centuries, it was not the first planet a space robot had visited. On December 14, 1962, NASA's *Mariner 2* became the first space mission to complete a flyby of another planet. It came within 21,644 miles (34,833 km) of Venus. Venus is easier to reach than Mars because it's closer to Earth.

CHAPTER 5

Asteroids and Comets

Planets and their moons are the biggest objects orbiting the sun. But there are also billions of small rocky asteroids and frozen icy **comets**. Asteroids and comets are the material that is left over from when the sun and planets formed. They are all over 4.5 billion years old. Asteroids and comets hold important clues that can help scientists answer questions about how Earth and the other planets formed. To search for these clues, NASA has sent robots to flyby, orbit, and land on asteroids and comets.

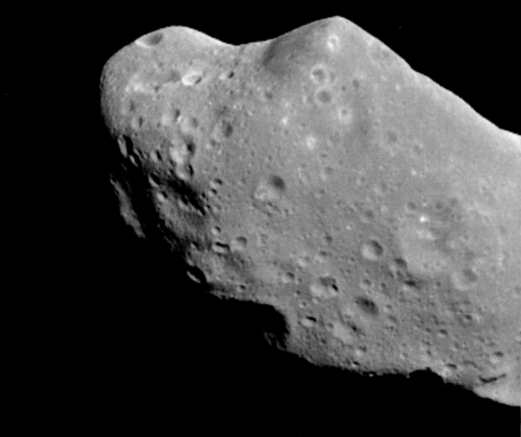

In 1993 while on its way to Jupiter, the *Galileo* spacecraft flew by an asteroid named Ida. *Galileo* sent pictures back to scientists on Earth. One of the pictures showed an amazing discovery. Ida has a tiny moon orbiting it! Scientists named the moon Dactyl. Dactyl was the first moon of an asteroid ever discovered. Since then scientists have discovered moons orbiting hundreds of different asteroids.

comet—a ball of rock and ice that orbits the sun

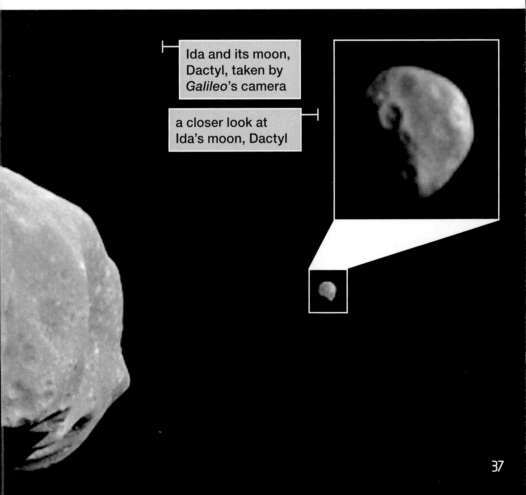

Ida and its moon, Dactyl, taken by *Galileo*'s camera

a closer look at Ida's moon, Dactyl

On February 14, 2000, the NASA mission *NEAR* became the first robot to explore an asteroid close up. Scientists built the solar-powered *NEAR* robot to be an orbiter. *NEAR* traveled to the asteroid Eros. Eros is called a near-Earth asteroid. It is one of about 10,000 asteroids that come very close to our planet. Scientists want to learn more about near-Earth asteroids. Someday they may need to stop one from hitting Earth.

The yellow circle shows where *NEAR* touched down on the asteroid Eros.

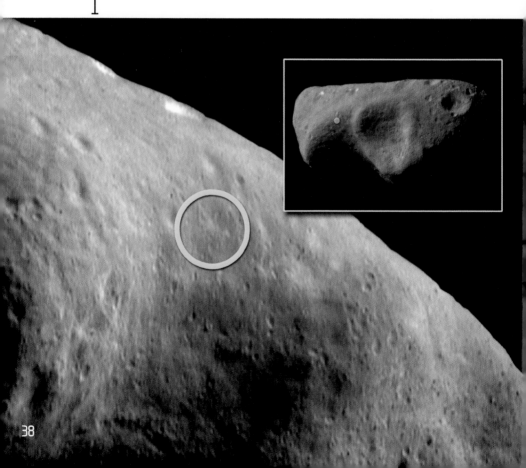

After studying Eros for a year, scientists came up with a plan to get very close-up pictures of the asteroid. Even though *NEAR* didn't have any legs, they wanted to try to land it on the asteroid. Using two of the solar panels as legs, they lowered it very slowly. It took 4 hours for the little orbiter to drop down and land, but it worked perfectly. NASA had turned an orbiter into a lander! The little robot worked for a few more days, sending scientists information about the rocks and soil on the surface of the asteroid.

WHO WORKS ON SPACE ROBOTS?

Many scientists work together on each space robot mission. One such scientist is Dr. Lucy McFadden. Dr. McFadden works at NASA's Goddard Space Flight Center in Greenbelt, Maryland. She was a member of the teams for the *NEAR*, *Deep Impact*, and *Dawn* missions. Dr. McFadden has studied asteroids, comets, the moon, Mars, meteorites, and the giant moons of Jupiter. She has also traveled to Antarctica to collect meteorite samples from the ice fields.

What are comets made of? What are they like on the inside? Will they break apart if we try to block one from hitting Earth? To help answer these questions, NASA built different robots to explore comets. One of these robots was a solar-powered flyby robot named *Stardust*. In 1999 NASA sent *Stardust* on a seven-year mission to fly very close to a comet. *Stardust* would also collect some of the dust coming off the comet.

In 2006 *Stardust* came back past Earth and dropped off a capsule with the dust inside. Now scientists on Earth are studying the comet dust. They have discovered that the dust in the comet was once very hot before it was frozen inside the icy comet billions of years ago. How this happened is still a mystery.

NASA designed the *Deep Impact* robot to study the inside of a comet named Tempel 1. As the robot was flying by Tempel 1 on July 4, 2005, it released an 800-pound (360-kg) cannon ball. The comet smashed into the cannon ball going more than 23,000 miles (37,000 km) per hour. Scientists learned that this comet had some dust inside, but less ice than they thought. Scientists also learned that Tempel 1 is mostly empty space inside. It's like a sponge with a lot of holes.

Rosetta's camera took this photo of a comet on April 26, 2015.

Another spacecraft named *Rosetta* began studying a different comet in 2014. *Rosetta* is a two-part mission. *Rosetta* has an orbiter that is going around the comet and also a small lander that is on the surface. Scientists are using *Rosetta* to study what happens to a comet as it gets closer to the sun. Sunlight is heating up the comet and turning some of its ice into gas, giving it a long tail. *Rosetta* will follow the comet until 2016 to study how the comet's tail changes.

CHAPTER 6

Robots of the Future

Space robots help scientists answer questions about the solar system. Many times the answers lead to more questions. To help answer these new questions, scientists are building even better robots to explore space.

One new question is, "Are any creatures alive in the deep ocean on Jupiter's moon Europa?" NASA is making plans to send a swimming, fishlike robot into Europa's ocean to find out. Another question is, "How do the empty holes inside a comet form?" NASA scientists think a slithering snakelike robot could go into the holes to explore.

Sometime in the future, people will travel to Mars. When they go, they will bring robots with them to help explore. Scientists are already working on some of those robots. The robots look a little bit like astronauts. They are called robonauts. Astronauts working on the **International Space Station** are testing a robonaut. It helps them with experiments and with jobs outside the space station. When astronauts are ready to go to Mars, they will explore it together with robonauts. Imagine all the different ways they could explore together!

International Space Station—a place where astronauts live and work in space

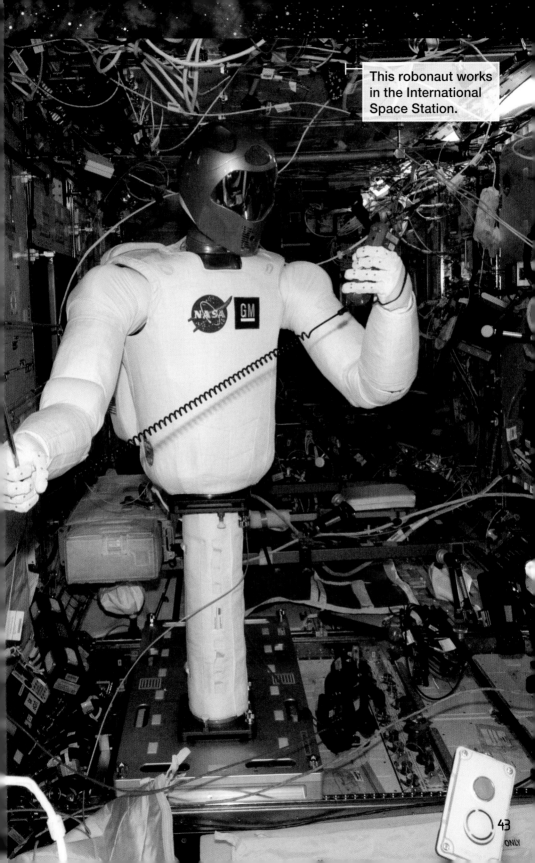

This robonaut works in the International Space Station.

An orbiter named *JUNO* is on its way to Jupiter. *JUNO* will arrive at Jupiter in 2016. It will study the strong gravity of the giant planet. Some scientists think that Jupiter may have a core ten times more massive than Earth. Scientists will use information from *JUNO* to help figure out if this is true. By learning about Jupiter's interior, scientists may be able to determine how Jupiter formed billions of years ago.

an artwork of *OSIRIS-Rex* approaching the asteroid Bennu

A NASA mission named *OSIRIS-Rex* will launch in 2018. *OSIRIS-Rex* will head for an asteroid named Bennu. When *OSIRIS-Rex* gets to Bennu, a long robotic arm will reach out and scoop up rocks and soil from the surface. NASA will then bring these asteroid samples back to Earth for scientists to study. Scientists hope to learn more about how Earth formed by studying the pieces of Bennu.

NASA is also building the next Mars rover. It will launch in 2020. The new rover will land on Mars as *Curiosity* did, with the sky crane, but in a different spot. Right now scientists are studying the surface of Mars to find the best place to send the new rover to search for signs of life.

This artwork shows the 2016 scheduled arrival of *Juno* at Jupiter.

Glossary

asteroid (AS-tuh-royd)—a large rock that travels through space

atmosphere (AT-muhss-fihr)—the layer of gases that surrounds some planets, dwarf planets, and moons

atom (AT-uhm)—a piece of matter in its smallest form

comet (KOM-uht)—a ball of rock and ice that orbits the sun

core (KOR)—the inner part of a planet or dwarf planet that is made of metal or rock

erosion (i-ROH-zhuhn)—wearing away of rock or soil by wind, water, or ice

generator (JEN-uh-ray-tur)—a machine that converts energy into electricity

International Space Station (in-tur-NASH-uh-nuhl SPAYSS STAY-shuhn)—a place where astronauts live and work in space

lander (LAND-uhr)—a spacecraft that lands on an object to study the surface

mineral (MIN-ur-uhl)—a solid substance often found in rocks or soil

nuclear (NOO-klee-ur)—having to do with the energy created by splitting atoms

orbiter (OR-bit-ur)—a spacecraft that orbits a planet or other space objects

pole (POHL)—the northernmost or southernmost point on a planet

probe (PROHB)—a small vehicle used to explore objects in outer space

rover (ROH-vur)—a small vehicle moved by remote control

solar panel (SOH-lur PAN-uhl)—a flat surface that collects sunlight and turns it into power

Critical Thinking Using the Common Core

1. What things have humans on Earth learned from studying the information gathered by space robots? Why is it important for humans to study outer space? (Key Idea and Details)

2. Compare and contrast a lander and a rover. What is the benefit of a lander if it can only land but not move? (Craft and Structure)

3. Imagine you worked for NASA and your job was to build a robot to explore a new planet. Which kind of robot would you send first? (Integration of Knowledge and Ideas).

Read More

Furstinger, Nancy. *Robots in Space.* Minneapolis: Lerner Publications, 2015.

Maxwell, Scott, and **Catherine Chambers.** *Mars Rover Driver.* The Coolest Jobs on the Planet. Chicago: Raintree, 2014.

Rusch, Elizabeth. *The Mighty Mars Rovers: The Incredible Adventures of Spirit and Opportunity.* Boston: Houghton Mifflin Books for Children, 2012.

Internet Sites

FactHound offers a safe, fun way to find Internet sites related to this book. All of the sites on FactHound have been researched by our staff.

Here's all you do:

Visit *www.facthound.com*

Type in this code: 9781491441633

 Check out projects, games and lots more at
www.capstonekids.com

Index